The Outward Edge of Joy
A Life in Poems

The Collected Work of
Chavatzelet Lillian Levin Kahn

Collected and edited by
Shulamit Kahn

Garnet Star Publishing
Boston

The Outward Edge of Joy

"Move on," an inner
Voice repeats.
Move on, move on
To other feats.
To other people,
Others' lives,
To touch the
Outward edge of joy
But not to taste it
Whole, full-blown ...

-- from "We're Always In Between,"
page 104

Contents

Lillian and her family, 1956. Left to right: Rabbi Eli J. Kahn,
Judy, Lillian; Rachelle, David, Shulamit

Chronology

Chicago, Illinois	July 17, 1917
Married Rabbi Eli Jerome Kahn, May 6, 1943	
Columbus, Georgia	1943 - 1945
Indiana Harbor, Indiana	1945 - 1957
Judy born	1946
Rachelle born	1948
Shulamit born	1950
David born	1952
Edmonton, Alberta, Canada	1957 - 1960
St. Paul, Minnesota	1960 - 1968
Rochester, Minnesota	1968 - 1970
Clarksburg, West Virginia	1970 - 1974
Johnstown, Pennsylvania	1974 - 1977
Temple Hills, Maryland	1977 - 1980
Potomac, Maryland	1980 - 1981
Sarnia, Ontario, Canada	1981 - 1983
Corpus Christi, Texas	1983 - 1984
New Castle, Pennsylvania	1984 - 1990
Scottsdale, Arizona	1990 - 1992
Skokie, Illinois	1992 - 2013
Chicago, Illinois	2014 ...

1

Lillian Levin, 1941

Introduction

by her daughter, Shulamit Kahn

We were closing out my Mother's house. I asked her, "Don't you want anything in the house to bring to your assisted living apartment? Paintings? Small Tzotchkes?" My Mother refused, saying that nothing in her house was really worth anything, was really worth keeping, except, she added, the small suitcase in the study marked "my materials."

"My materials" turned out to be poems. A suitcase full of poems. Typed and untyped. Few dated. Many of the typed poems were there in more than one version: various reincarnations, rewrites, edits over the years. In Scottsdale in the early 1990s, my Mom took a poetry course and revived some of the poems she felt were her best, trying to improve them. But few seemed to have been first written then.

Looking back at the age of 97, she doesn't remember writing many of these poems, nor can she imagine what she was thinking, or feeling, when she wrote most of those poems. It happened a life ago, a world ago. She always felt that her poems were not good enough.

My Mother wrote very little besides poetry. The little bit I found included the self-reflection that "Frankly, prose is not my forte and I have always felt stiff and sterile when contemplating it."

Truth to tell, few of these poems were ever likely

to get published in the *New Yorker*, at least not in recent decades. Many seem to be the kind of poetry popular in the first half of the twentieth century, when educated people thought that sonnets were the height of intellectualism, when 'tis and 'twere were in common usage, when poems all rhymed.

But many of these poems really do tell the story of my Mother's inner life.

Some of the poems are reflections on nature. Many are about seeing holiness in nature and in the world around her. Many indicate how deeply she was enveloped in the world of Jewish holidays and traditions.

The most revealing to me, however, are the poems on family, on moving, and the ones on her own sadness. (See especially the chapter "The Glass Half Empty.") None seem to have been written any time from the mid-1990s and on, when she watched her husband slipping into Alzheimer's and then passing away. Instead, I am guessing that they came from earlier bouts of depression that came and went throughout her life.

My Father was a peripatetic Rabbi, moving often. The chronology of where they lived precedes this introduction, hinting to when a poem might be written. An Orthodox Jew in his personal beliefs, my Father was best suited as a Rabbi for people who were not necessarily Orthodox themselves but who felt Jewish, whom he could encourage to get closer to tradition. He was a great success in Indiana Harbor, beloved and loving every minute of it. All four children were born there. The friendships my Mother made there were the most enduring, continuing until the people passed away. After that whole community disintegrated with the rapid segregation of the East Chicago area, they never found another synagogue that they truly loved.

The congregation in St. Paul was the second longest stint. At some point, however, my father's contract was not renewed. One reason may have been that my father experienced mild epilepsy there, which surfaced after a blow from a large falling icicle, but probably originated when he jumped out of the Yeshiva[1] window in his teens. But probably the reason he had to leave St Paul was that the synagogue started going through an identity crisis, like many others of its ilk did. Indeed, the period from the late 1960s through the 1990s was a time when my Father's niche, traditional (masorti[2]) Judaism, was dwindling. To the right of this niche were the very orthodox congregations where everyone was shomer Shabbat[3] (or posed as such). These synagogues were not attractive to my father, nor he to them. As one example: These synagogues did not want sermons, they wanted divrei Torah.[4] My father loved giving sermons. To the left of my Dad's niche were congregations

---

1 *Yeshiva*, religious school

2 The *Masorti* movement, between Orthodox and Conservative.

3 To be *Shomer Shabbat* is to keep the Sabbath in the traditional manner.

4 *Divrei Torah*, commentaries on the Torah portion of the week.

that were becoming increasingly egalitarian and chose which traditions to keep and which not to. Women contributing equally in services was a line my Father would not cross.

As the chronology preceding this introduction shows, every few years my mother packed up everything and moved it to a new city, a new home. The same furniture, a little more damaged with every move, re-created the same living room in small communities across the country, from Temple Hills, Maryland, to Scottsdale, Arizona, with stints in Pennsylvania, Ontario, West Virginia and Texas. Marry a Rabbi, see North America.

My mother never really had a choice in the matter. Once, she did stay in the previous city for an extra half year (with our dear cousin Rochelle) to work long enough for a government pension. Except for that, she packed and moved and unpacked, recreating home after home, losing the energy needed to make new really close friends.

While her children were at home, they kept her busy and generally happy. However, the poignant poem written when her youngest David first went to school showed how short lived that period was. And in poem after poem, she seems to feel that she has failed her daughters, made some fatal mistake that she didn't really identify. I am never sure which of her daughters she felt most sad about. It could have been any of us, for different reasons. I for one believe that she managed to do a pretty good job raising her kids, judging from the people they later became. But of course, I am prejudiced there.

Another genre of my Mother's writings is not included here – except for a few introductory poems. These were plays, combining prose, poetry and song, which she composed in her role of program manager of many of their congregations. There was one on the occasion of Israel's 10th anniversary, one for the holiday of Shavuot, etc. These are long and not very revealing of her inner feelings so are not included here.

I could write a longer introduction, explaining my guesses about some of the poems' back stories. I will not do that, allowing the poems to speak for themselves. Moreover, this would not be the majority of the poems. Most of the poems were probably written before I was aware of her as a person, many even before I was born. I write dates where I have some sense of where (and therefore when) they must have been written. I am guessing that many of the poems that I found untyped had been written earliest, before I was born.

Enjoy,

Shulamit Kahn

On Friendship, Love, and Other Emotions

Rabbi Moshe Zev Kahn with Lillian, 1956

Thoughts at Random (c. 1960)

For years, many or few, as you view a lifetime, I have been disturbed by thoughts -- thoughts deep and superficial, thoughts morose or heartening. But ever has there been the urge to record them in some manner, to pen them in some way, to be part of the Universal Intelligence in some infinitesimal act of creation. The mind murmurs, "Write;" the heart echoes, "Write;" so that one's existence on this earth will not be completely sterile, so that the curse of spiritual barrenness will not haunt the latter days.

To this end, I have determined to set down these "Thoughts at Random," but not random thoughts, which have accumulated in the now dusty files of my memory or my notebook or are presently intruding themselves into my thinking. After 17 years as a Rabbi's wife in communities stretching from the stifling, confining red-clay valley of the Chatahoochee to the chilly but invigorating expanses of Canada's Alberta; from the acrid, chemical environs of the Hoosier steel cities to the comparatively farm-fresh atmosphere of central Minnesota, I suddenly feel the desire to sermonize, to unfold layered thoughts in poetry or prose.

Let the reader challenge or contradict, let him agree or commiserate, let him but read these outpourings of my mind and soul, and I will be forever grateful. I will offer thanks to him and to my Father in Heaven for deeming me worthy to clothe these dead words in the sinews of the living page. May the heritage of my maternal grandfather[1] and my husband's father[2], both of blessed memory, serve me as inspiration and guide.

---

1 Rabbi Yekusial Segal
2 Rabbi Moshe Zev Kahn

Old Friends

The friends of our youth are friends indeed
Though far and wide they roam,
Should you encounter them, as you may,
They signal a breath of home.

Their presence unravels a vision of joy,
Of happiness pure and serene,
Of a smile or glance of enveloping warmth,
Of a joyful remembered scene.

No rude disenchantment clouds the bright view,
Their flaws have dissolved in the past,
Only the pleasures of friendship and love
Abide and endure to the last.

Lillian with friends in Indiana Harbor, 1954

Pause

Won't you come into my parlor
From out the howling winds.
Rest and drink a cup of tea
And chat, and warm your limbs.

Remain in friendship's glow, till you
Have gathered strength to face
The heavy winter snow and cold,
The bleak, foreboding space.

Then travel on, performing deeds
That lift your fellow-man,
And when your burdens weigh you down,
Return and stop again.

Lillian's tea set.

14

Reward

(c. 1970s, Clarksburg)

Strange, odd, strange,
Alone, alone, alone.
Why so sad and solitary?
Why so somber? Come be merry.

Befriend a single groping soul,
Offer friendship, comfort, goal.
In concern for fellow's fate
You'll forget your lonely state.

Alone

I walked alone
And sensed the dark--
I feared what was not there;

I walked with you
And saw the stars
As moonbeams filled the air.

II
I walked alone
And was afraid
Of shadow and of night;

I walked with you
In hope and trust,
And all the world shone bright.

Sonnet To You
(c. 1960, Edmonton)

There's a lilt in my step
And a song on my lips.
There's a smile from the depths of my soul.
Though youth's fresh-blown ardor
That bloomed in the past
Is gone, as the years take their toll,
Yet the warm, flowing fervor
That fuses our hearts,
Is surely love's glorious goal.

Eli and Lillian, August 1944

To Lesha

Revel youth while you are young,
Your happiness embrace at once,
Don't let the doubts of age and strain
Misguide you to a path of pain.

Rejoice, dear one, while yet the bloom
Of youth and joy are in your grasp.
Discard the fears of coming years,
Set your goals for lofty tasks.

Lesha Bellows Greengus the bride, Eva Kahn Eli's mother, Sam Greengus the groom, and Uncle Abba Hillel Skolnick.

The Post Lady

I saw her knock upon a door
Which, very slowly, opened wide.
An older woman stood inside,
She smiled and gestured as she spoke,
"Come in, come in. There's mail for me?"

The postal lady from her bag
Withdrew some letters
Where she stood
And waited for a signature
Needed on a piece of mail.

With true concern, she kindly spoke:
"I hope today you are feeling well
Enough to venture to the gate,
I'll help you cross the narrow step
Where you can sit."

Despite the fact she might be late
To finish off her scheduled route,
This postal lady's clock stood still
So she could help
Her customer.

When You're Away

When you are here
You don't have to speak
Yet your presence pervades every room.

But when you're away,
The emptiness grows,
Engulfs me with shudders
Of doubt and of fear;

A silence so strong,
Its power intense
Like a grasping vise
Stealthily enfolding,
So the void chokes
And I gasp for your pure air.

Eli and Lillian, about 1984

A Past Love

Do not pass this way again,
Your face belongs to former years,
Your love, once flaming, now is charred.

But when I heard your voice today,
And saw you standing in the flesh,
Memory tapped a spidered door--

Roused from Rip Van Winkle sleep
Emotions that were better dead.
Buried, hidden in the past.

So do not walk this way again
To stir the leaves that forgot
And lure the spirits from the grave.

In The Lunchroom

The lunchroom was almost empty,
Most of the counters were clean;
There near an open window
At a table loaded with books,
They sat conversing intently
Ignoring the sweet-scented breeze;.
She with a small cap of orange
Tight over black-flowing locks,
He in a gaudy plaid shirt,
His hair the color of sand.
Her black head bowed towards his sandy,
Gesticulating one to the other,
Their fingers locked often and warmly,
They saw no one about them,
Oblivious to anyone near.

Were they talking of testing or classes
Or of meeting for future delight?
From their manner no one could fathom
Their words
Or the depth of their thoughts.

Anger

Anger out of all proportion,
Biting, caustic, curdling, sharp,
Anger more than of this moment;
Anger for the lost directions,
For the paths which were not trod,
Anger for the fleeting chances,
Unseized before they disappeared;
Anger for the unseen choices,
Untapped sources screened from view
Perhaps revealing brighter sharper visions,
Hidden, nobler, yearned-for goals.
Anger burst and blazed unbridled
When the fuse blew out last night.

What Have I Done?

What have I done?
That hatred strong
As lion's claws on pygmy's neck
Crush me down and make me faint.
What have I done?

What have I done?
To sow mistrust,
Deceits, disgust and treachery
That scorches like a firebrand.
What have I done?

What have I done?
To earn the scorn
That blurs my eyes, constricts my brain,
Chills and shudders rack my frame
What have I done?

Hate

The stark, mad winds of hate can chill you
Though you're dressed against the cold.
Only inner strength can fill you
With the courage to warm the soul.

The Adventure

"Life is an adventure",
I heard the poet say,
So seize the reins and stay the course
And live from day to day.

Wedding dinner 1943. Left to right: Lillian, Eli; Eli's brother
Sol Kahn with date; unidentified couple; Nate Roseman with
Lillian's sister Ruth Roseman

Transfusion

(probably written to comfort a congregant)

Trickle, trickle, drop on drop,
The blood must flow; don't let it stop!
Slowly, slowly, not so fast,
Let it trickle, it must last.

Do not stir, don't dare to move,
Don't touch that needle as it moves.
Only patience, plodding, sure,
Will keep your body still, secure.

Seconds, minutes, hours long,
That blood will make your body strong.
Suffer, bear, be patient, please,
Soon you'll have relief with ease.

Endless was the patience needed,
Hurrah, behold you have succeeded!
The seconds dragged, the minutes, hours,
One by one like petaled flowers,
The nurse glides softly in to see,
The vigil's ended! Now, you're free!

The Apartment (Or, A Study in Sadness)
(Helping a community member)

Seeking a modest apartment,
She came to us for help;
Dressed in blue jeans and a blouse
Of sallow brown with raveling sleeves,
Spotted, faded, patched and worn,
Apologizing for her looks--
"My sister's hippie clothes," she said.

Her child clung closely to her side.
"His father's somewhere far away,
A soldier lost in Vietnam,
Missing now for many years,
His family did not, would not know me.
'Let's not make trouble,' said my mother."

She herself a grown-up child
With smiling teeth but vapid eyes.
"I don't want to ask for help,
I live at Mother's with my son,
I pay her when she babysits,
I only want another place
Because my sister quarrels so
And mother always takes her side.
We're crowding someone else's space,
My lonely child and I."

My own responsibility I know,
I cannot pay too much,
But I would like to live alone
And leave the arguments behind,
Please help me find a place to live
I, together with my child."
The sadness slipped away a bit,
"He really is the most beautiful,
Most beautiful in all this town."

A Unified Whole
(Untyped)

On TV this morning
I heard a stunning talk
Of nuclei and atoms
Electrons and protons
And rocks from ancient time
Whose lines hold untold secrets
Of the universe and time
Before the dawn of man.

Particles and forces
Which magnetize or repel.

G-d is subtle but not malicious
The principle is simple
A unified whole.

On Family

The Sabbath Twist
(c. 1984)

When I rolled the ropes of Hallah[1]
To form into a braid,
The image of my mother
Appeared to share my task.
I saw her hands before me
Now moving back and forth,
Braids of twisted beauty
Appearing on the board.
When I rolled the strands of Hallah,
My mother came in view
To stand so still beside me
And guide my hands once more.

1   Hebrew word for Sabbath bread

Our Children
(Corpus Christi, Texas, 1984)

They're gone, all gone,
Were they here?
When did they come?
And when did they leave?
They left no trace,
No aura,
No sound,
They left no print,
No word,
No act,
Did we place no stamp upon them?
Did we lack for strength and firmness?
Did we flinch from guides and precepts?
Were we weak and too permissive?

What's your message, oh, my children?
Can you answer face to face?
Have I lost you, all my children,
To the future, have I lost you?
What's your answer, oh, my children?
Would we could communicate!
What's the message, all my children,
That you failed to leave behind?

Across the Ocean
(Untyped)

My mother and those with her
Who came across the ocean
To an unknown land
Were surely daring and courageous
Even though they had no choice.
Grandfather went and said
"Come," and she came.
A young woman
Shy and soft-spoken
And ripe for life.
So she was happy to find a place
And remain
Not to roam and seek new horizons
She had already crossed a tremendous one.

Lillian's parents, Shlomo and Devora
Levin, about 1960.

My Bubbe[1]

My thoughts roll back to Bubbe dear,
Whom, sad to say, I never knew
Because she died in prime of life
Serving those less fortunate,
The sick, the hungry and the poor,
Those who fell between the cracks.

When she was only thirty-two
And famine stalked a neighbor's house,
She rose before a winter's dawn,
And in the bitter, biting cold
Stole with milk and bread and cheese,
The stealth of one who hides his deed,
So no one in the neighbor's house
Would know what angel left the fare
And silver, too, to nourish those
With bodies wracked from hunger pangs.

With but a thin, grey shawl as shield
She shivered in the acrid frost,
Pneumonia seized her, laid her low;
Scarcely did the doctor come,
When gasping low, she breathed her last,
For fever, sweat and pain proved fatal
To her selfless, pious deed.

---

1   *Bubbe* is Yiddish for Grandmother

So before a fortnight passed,
They buried her in graveyard's gloom,
Nevermore to spread good deeds,
Nor silently to serve a need.

Dear Bubbe, gone so many years,
Alive, I see you in my dreams,
Though in the flesh I knew you not,
I proudly bear your hallowed name
To me your spirit's fresh as breath
I pray it may beat strong in me,
And guide me on to noble tasks,
Concern for sick, for poor, for weak
Bubbe dear, I miss you so,
When the past lights up my view.

Lillian's mother Devora holding
Judy Kahn

I Wonder Why
(Untyped, 1977)

Last night I saw my mother
Talked with her about
An everyday matter
Real as truth
Then I remembered
In my dream
I knew she was dead
Gone three years
But she was oh so real
As life as truth
Last night I saw my mother.
I wonder why.

A Child

(Untyped, ca. 1953)

Despair and sadness governed me
And shame, that no creative wage
Had shaped the markings of my pen;
Then darting through the layers of grief
A sound, a voice, a baby's cry
My son was calling close at hand
The child's sweet sob of need and love
Compelling proof of re-creation
Revived my spirit, hope and pride
Dispelled my self-recrimination
Bestirred my sorely fainting soul.

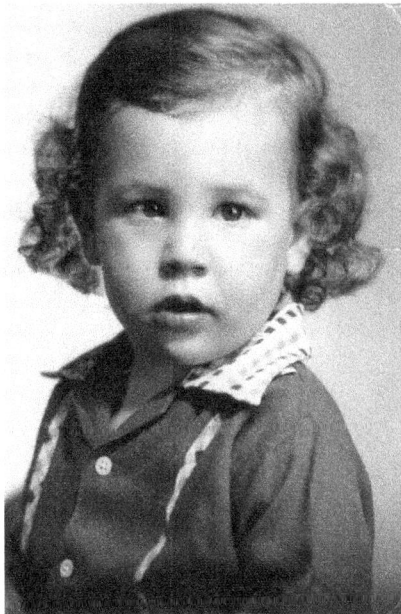

David at three years old

Daughters

O my daughters, lovely daughters,
Would that you could hear my cry
Of the promise of your greatness,
Of achievement and success,
Of your scaling boundless barriers,
Reaching goals no one could guess.

Did I burden you with baggage
That was mine alone to heave?
Did I shoulder you with burdens,
Solely mine to dare retrieve?

Did I make demands upon you
As I visioned goal on goal?
My sweet daughters, I have wronged you,
Sorely bitter is my soul!

Rachelle, Lillian, Shu, Judy, Passover 1964

My Father

I never dreamt about my Father
But tonight I saw him in my dream
I lost him when a walk collapsed
Again I saw him straight and sharp
Looking not like memory had him
Pictured in my mind.
My father, yet a stranger too.
What indeed could this dream mean?

A Puzzle

I bore children, but they're not mine,
I loved them and I mothered them,
I guided them but to no goal.
The principles I thought I taught,
Were dissipated in a web,
A maze of inconsistencies.

My child, my child, I loved you so,
Where are you lost, where did you go?
Your form I see, your pretty face,
But like the shadow nights erase
Your spirit flees and is effaced,
Your eyes a tortured sadness show.

My child, first-born of love and woe,
My lovely child, where did you go?

Lillian with Judy

Farewell
(ca. 1957)

It's a strange feeling
Leaving my son in school all day
To study, to eat,
To take care of his own
Worldly needs.

Not to see him
From nine to four
Not to hear his shouts at play
He is no longer a baby,
He's a big boy now.

Melancholy overwhelms me
I think how strange it is
Slowly loosening the apron strings
Reflection runs rampant

David 1959

Farewell my son, my little boy
Farewell fore'er to babyhood
Now you go to school my son
As every normal young man should
Your mother's sad, holds back her tears
She can't, of course,
Hold back the years.

To Rachelle

My daughter Rachelle's
A violent gal
Her anger is bottomless,
Her laughter as well.

She acts like a child
Boisterous and wild
Though strong as an Amazon
By fear she's beguiled.

From depths of despair
To ecstasy so rare
She's quite unpredictable
A curse -- and a prayer!

Daughter Rachelle

44

My Lost Child
(1991)

Abandoned by G-d?
She abandoned Him.
There's no anchor, no more
Nor a tangible shore.

No goal worth achieving
No bright future beckoning
To where does she turn
To what does she reach?

Ginger Lost

(A poem to be read to children. St. Paul, before 1965)

To think that one
Can so become
Attached unto a dog!
A creature dumb,
Yet anyone
Of us would swear
She's not.

The Bible teaches
Pity for creatures
Such as our little dog.
We hope the one
Who took her home
Will show her
Just such love.[1]

Kids with Ginger. Left to right:
Judy, Shu, Ginger, Rachelle

---

1   Ginger was found by a neighbor who got our
phone number from her license.

Dear G-d
(Untyped)

What do we do
When truths become plain
Our children in pain
In silent despair.

Our heart cries with love
To reach out and share
To comfort and hug
Fearing to break down
And weaken the pluck
Our child must display
To soften the blow
To shield from the hurt
To guard against pity
A burden too great
To bear and support
So let her be silent
Let her turn inward
To reach for the strength
Her sorrow now seeks.

Eons and Ages and Centuries Ago

(Untyped, reflecting on the divorce of someone near to her)

Eons and ages and centuries ago
Our life was more placid, more calm and serene.
The tensions were minor
Living was bright
'Til dark slime of scandal
Oozed into view.
Staining and splattering
And shattering the scene.

Devotion and love, punctured and shed
Abandoned are children and wife and belief
Surrendered to pleasure
To "I alone matter"
Who spawned this Jekyll,
This changeling, this freak?
Once husband concerned
And father who cared.
Destroyed now shared goals
And family and home.
Like Humpty Dumpty
Crashed and was gone.

One More Month Plus Six Full Days

(1971 when David was studying in Israel)

One more month plus six full days
And then we'll see you once again.
Eighteen months is very long
In a brief lifetime of eighteen years,
I think you've really grown apart
And live an alien life to us.

We love you and we long to see
The changes school and time have made.
But I fear you'll tire soon
Of seeing us, our narrow life
Our shallow likes, what gives us joy
Our lack of substance and of depth.
I know my son you've grown apart.
In thought and spirit, deeds and words
Never to return.

With David near the time of the poem,
when he went to study in Israel

49

Waiting

It's seventeen months, over five hundred days,
Since last I saw your face,
It's seventeen months,
    more than five hundred days,
Since I last talked to you.

I got your tape,
I viewed a slide,
Whereon your form was stamped.
I read the words
Your letters showed
From where your image peaked,
And I was satisfied.

Now your coming time draws near,
And every day's a year,
Every hour's a month or more
Fraught with anxious fears.

The phone that rang so late last night
Didn't startle me,
I laid awake in shivering hope
That this would be the day.

I kept myself from rest and sleep
Until the break of dawn,
Perhaps you caught the plane this week
And would arrive quite soon.

You didn't come, you didn't call,
Anxiety grows fierce,
No longer is it self-contained,
It overspills my thoughts.

I cannot sleep,
I cannot think,
I'm tense, immobilized,
The minutes – hours,
The hours – days,
And nothing satisfies.

Yesterday?

As though you hadn't been abroad
For more than eighteen months,
As though you had just shut the door,
Yesterday or the day before,
You walked straight in and took your place,
Where you had stood before.
The days retreated and we were back
In that summer two years ago.

And yet --you seemed to be someone else,
Who nodded and answered and looked.
The boy that had traveled
Ten thousand miles
Away from home and school,
Was not the young man
Who stood at the door,
But a youth we have never
Encountered before.

I didn't think you'd stay so long
And carve yourself a niche,
In which to lodge and hold on tight
Become estranged from friend and home
Reluctant to return.

So be it. For the time has passed
When we could call a halt.
And who is it that really knows
The path that you should tread.
Only you and you alone
Turn then to where it leads.

Faith

Meditation

For peace of mind,
For calm of heart,
For nerves unfrayed by tension,
Direct my gaze to Thee, dear G-d,
For succor and redemption.

For joy of years,
For strength of mind,
For gifts too myriad to mention,
Light my path to Thee, O G-d,
For guidance and salvation.

Plea

Forgive us now, O G-d, we pray,
For sins committed every day,
For wrongs we've done our fellow-man,
For dreams of evil
Thoughts of shame.
Cleanse our souls and make them pure,
So that we may Thy laws obey.

I Pray
(c. 1965)

O G-d, to Thee alone I turn,
Bowed by worry, grief and fear.
Fellow man is mean, unfeeling
Only Thou willst lend an ear.

Gather me unto Thy bosom.
Soothe my suffering aching heart;
Comfort me and give me wisdom
Not to heed the insult's dart.

Many are the wounds I carry,
Scars of anguish make me faint;
Only Thou, my Heavenly Father,
Can assuage my grievous pain.

Beyond Space
(c. 1960s)

Beyond the cold horizons
And Van Allen's belts,
Beyond the floating worlds
With all their flashing stars;

Beyond the reach of knowledge,
Above the realm of man,
The still, small voice of G-d is heard,[1]
The Master of the Plan.

Artist's depiction of Van Allen's belt, a donut-shaped zone
of highly energized charged particles trapped at high
altitudes in the magnetic field surrounding the planet
Earth, discovered by physicist James Van Allen in 1958.
Picture courtesy of the U.S. National Aeronautics and Space
Administration (NASA).

---

1   Kings I: 19:11-12

Paradox

Sanctuaries that rise to heights,
Temples that dazzle men,
Where Thy still small Voice is drowned
By organs' crashing din.

Gorgeous woods and brilliant tones
Evoke our joy and pride;
But where Thy Spirit finds no niche,
Thy Presence stands aside.

A Prayer

Cause us, G-d, each night to rest
Beneath Thy sheltered grace.
Awaken us at morning's break
Invigorated for the pace
Of varied duties, tasks untold,
Though ever-mindful we,
That, if Thy Presence hovers near,
Quickened shall we be.

The Source

The mind of man to comprehend
And chart the obscure spheres
Attest to its divinity
Mocks him who scorns or jeers.

The more that is revealed of Thee,
The wiser we become,
For Thou alone Creator wast,
Before our world began.

Wonder

Dear G-d, your world's magnificent,
It moves the heart to tears.
The heights to which man may aspire
Expand with passing years.

Horizons that we cannot see
Today, will loom in sight
As vision and intelligence
Reveal your greater might.

The more we learn to comprehend,
The more there is to know.
Infinity is fathomless,
And daily, wonders grow!

I Call Upon My G-d

I call upon my G-d
Distressed by the superficialities of living
And He answers!

I turn my empty, listless soul
Devoid of inspiration and emotion
And He succors it!

I bare my listless
Lifeless form to him
And He resuscitates.

G-d is ever here
For those who seek Him.

Travelers

We're all uncertain travelers towards the future.
Some feel they surely know where they are going,
Some view each day with keen anticipation,
Some look ahead for challenge and excitement,
Some only seek security and quiet.

No matter what our goal, our aspiration,
What certainties that life has destined
This moment is the one that we must cherish.
The future still is far away, elusive,
Though towards it moves our mind, our
    thoughts, our being.

It is G-d's challenge thrown to all His children
That can ennoble or debase and crush them.
As *Ethics*[1] tells us: "Everything's predestined
And yet to each free choice, free will is given."
So as we slowly travel towards the future
We can give it meaning.
We can redeem ourselves and bring forth
    blessings.

---

[1]   *Ethics of the Fathers,* or *Pirkei Avot*

Refuge

Raging winds whirl round about,
Piercing, howling, raging winds.
I quake, I shrink, I shudder,
Their fierceness strikes me numb.

Only in Thee, my gentle G-d
Is refuge from the winds of fate
And from the blasts of mortal hate.

Comfort
(c. 1959)

Is it the different country
Or the strange temperament
Cooled by nature's frost and snow
That does not pulse at fellow creature's hurt
And does not flinch at someone else's shame.
Or is each so lost among the vastness
Afraid to voice his loneliness and pain?

Alone to Thee, I softly, gently whisper
And know though many creatures live on earth,
I can converse with You, My Heavenly Father,
Across eternal space I hear Your word.

I Wonder

The poet sings:
"If Winter comes
Can Spring be far behind?"
With promise, faith and prayer.

I know that in His goodness
G-d sends Springs
To quicken hearts,
Revive and resurrect.

But in the midst of
All this dormant hope,
Who will there be
When Nature wakes
To rise and shout?

Nature

Autumn Days in Minnesota
(c. 1960s)

The tinge of Fall is in the air,
The tang of burning leaves,
The zest that nippy mornings bring,
The gathering of sheaves.

The world of Nature beds itself
With bold, emblazoned strokes.
With fanfare flashing through the trees
The willows, sumacs, oaks.

As if to shout, "Though dormant soon
I peacefully shall lie
To gather strength, refresh myself
I sleep; I do not die.

Then wait for me through frost and snow
Through Winter's ice and gloom.
I shall arise before you know
And spring and love will bloom.

Soliloquy

Dear Lord, your world is radiant
From plains to snow-capped hills,
The azure, turquoise, purple, blue
Of lakes and streams and rills.

The mountain heights that scrape the sky,
The gray and golden sand,
The seas of green in summer's sun
The harvest of the land.

The riot of the orchard's hues
From fruits of every kind
Whose luscious nectar piques the taste
And subtly drugs the mind.

My gratitude for eyes that see
This dazzling loveliness,
And limbs that share this sense of joy,
Dear Lord, I'm truly blessed.

From a Plane

Pristine clouds,
Dazzling bright,
Calm, serene,
Crystal mounds,
Clear as light,
Airy mountains
Viewed in flight.

The Canadian Rockies
(c. 1958 untyped)

Mountains have character
They possess personalities
Mountains are distinctive
And have idiosyncrasies
Go see for yourself!
Pilot Mountain perched to all directions
The Sisters Three quite low, but each peak rises
Or Eisenhower Mountain -- bold and girthy
Like a rotund mister, five by five.
Forest acres by the tens of thousands
Cover some with a luxurious carpet
Others tower sharp and straight and tall
With many varied layers of gradation
Sharply marked by snow and ice and winter.

Shu and Judy in the
Canadian Rockies, 1958

The Lake
(early 1960s)

Serene and calm,
It soothes the soul.
And offers balm
To jagged nerves.
The lake
That softly laps and flows
Towards other shores
And gently taps out music scores.

Bring the same
Still peace
To me.
Beyond horizon's edge
I seek
The inspiration
For my toil.

Strange

Sometimes snow seems bleak and dreary
Like the heart that's weak and weary,
Sometimes it sparkles diamond-bright,
Buoys the soul in sheer delight.

Thaw

Cold and bleak,
Harsh and wild,
Ice and sleet,
Winter's child.

Shut the door,
Draw the blinds,
Shield your heart
From howling winds.

Sun appears
Bright and clear,
Golden guest,
Spirits soar.

Thaw without,
Warmth within,
Hearts unfold,
Spring again!

Forgive

(Published 25 Oct 1963 in St Paul Jewish News)

Forgive us now, O G-d, we pray,

For sins committed day by day,

For wrongs we've done our fellow-men

For dreams of evil

Thoughts of shame.

Cleanse our soul and make it pure.

So that we may thy Laws obey.

Who But G-d?

(Impressions of a Brief Visit to Banff and Lake Louise, 1959)

Who but G-d could have created the majesty of
    the towering bluff?
Who but G-d could have imbedded a stream of
    jeweled waters
In the shaggy crags of a mountainside?

Who but G-d has imprisoned a sapphire lake
In the heaving bosom of the cascading hills?

Who but G-d could have fashioned these mighty
    contours
And covered their precarious slopes with trees
    and snow?

Who indeed but the unique One,
And in His infinite goodness
He whispered some of the secrets
To the pride of creation -- Man!

For a Few Quick Minutes
(untyped)

When dawn overtakes night,
The scene is so breathtaking
So overwhelming
You want to stand motionless
In awe,
Seizing the moments
When the Eastern horizon
Begins to glow with color
And the rim of the sun
Is visible in outline
To the west, clouds and pall
And in the east, color,
Throughout clutching color
Ethereal orange stroked across the Eastern sky
By a magnanimous Creator
Dispensing from his storehouse
Strokes of heavenly orange
And streaming rapidly
Above a lone bird outlined
Against the contrasting sky.

In awe I stand
Desiring to hold fast this heavenly beauty—
Turning away for a brief moment
To respond to more mundane leads—
Returning to find the promise gone, disappeared
Replaced by day of unexciting dimensions.

Autumn Moods

Let's capture yet the thrill of spring
In autumn's vibrant airs,
Let's glory in the radiant hues,
Before the winter stirs.

Let's revel in the warmth of rust,
Of yellow, red and brown,
And fill our lungs with fresh sweet scents,
Before the snows come down.

Was it Yesterday?

(published in Scimitar and Song, *July 15 1962.*
On the rapid change from Winter to Spring in
Minnesota)

Was it yesterday, these walks were heaped
With mounds of gleaming, frozen snow?
Today the grass is sprouting forth
And trees and flowers grow!

Perhaps it was a white-laced dream
Piled high on street and lawn
That lingers now in memory.
All trace of winter's gone.

Strange, indeed, are Nature's ways,
Yet this we surely know:
As night greets day and young grow old,
So greens replace the snow!

Snowflakes
(for children)

Snowflakes flying,
Snowflakes running
Here and there,
Everywhere.
See them run,
See them fly,
In the air,
Through the sky.

Seize them,
Snatch them
As they run,
Catching them
Is breathless fun!

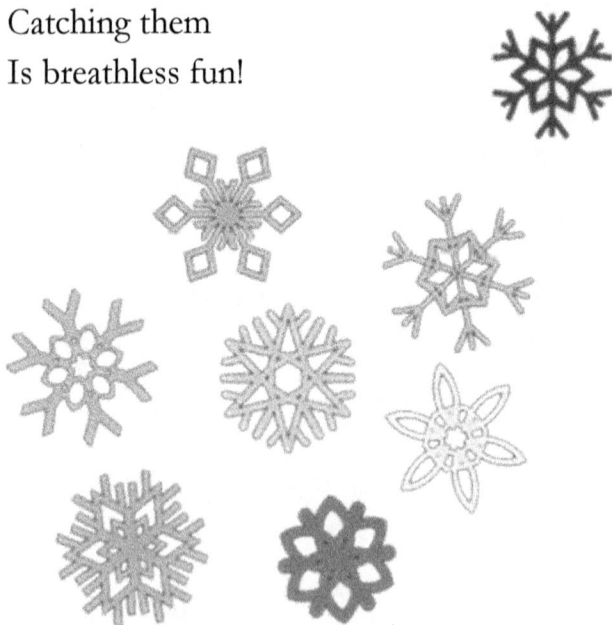

Snow

Crunch! Crunch! Crunch!
White, firm snow
Sleek as rock
Bright as light
Fresh as air
Greets your step
Flecks your foot
Wraps your walk.

As you rush
Through the frost
All is pure,
All is white.

Seize this hour,
Hold it fast,
Mint its seal,
Make it last.

Deep Winter

A curious bird upon the snow,
Foraging for food,
And lo, a scrap of bread appears
That looks so real and good?

Beyond's a squirrel looking on,
Quizzically absurd;
Is that the bread he stored away
That's manna for the bird?

Fragments

"It's going to rain again,"
You said,
But the sky was unveiling azure blue,
And an orange sun was peeking through.
What has incited your gloomy view?

Spring

Trees are blossoming,
Pink shoots peeking out from bare branches,
Green dots peppering the brown earth.
O, to be young again when Spring appears.

On Heaven's Runway

Looking skyward, as one might,
I saw a plane and bird in flight;
Both were soaring mountains high,
Both were racing through the sky;
The plane in predetermined path
With firm and rigid lifeless wings;
The bird a graceful, fluid form,
Of poetry its movement sings
As Heaven's boundless roads they skim,
The vibrant body, the mechanical limb,
Their flight a pointed message brings
Of Nature's wondrous, winged things.

At the Lake
(1960s)

Time slowly flows here,
It gently meanders
In ribbons of light,
Weaving through waters
In the lazy sun,
In the drifting boats.

Eli at Moraine Park, Illinois, 1987

A Day of Spring Lost in the Fall

A breeze murmuring
A soft blue sky
The grass clear green
Unflecked with brown.

A bouncing step
Replete with smiles;
Trees still sporting summer's leaves,
Fresh dry air, holding its breath,
For fear the day will disappear.
A day of Spring lost in the midst of Fall.

Along the Mississippi

Father of many waters,
Source of rivers and streams,
Many the autos cruising your banks,
Bursting with children and dreams.

Do they pause to recall
The grey, lazy days
Vividly pictured by Twain
Do they halt in their journey
To visualize scenes
Of the proud ones who peopled this plain?

I tarried a while
And I heard the clear tones
Of Tom and of Huck and of Twain;
Sad at the thought
That the sounds of the past,
Were lost in the roar of a train.

The Mississippi River at St. Paul, photo taken by Lillian, 1964

On Moving

The Time has Come

The time has come
For us again
To take our staff in hand
To find another stopping place
In traveling through the land.

Rabbi and Rebbitzin[1] with the Hebrew School graduating
class in St. Paul, mid 1960's

---

1   *The Rebbitzin*, the wife of the Rabbi, was expected to run
the school, the women's activities, and holiday events, without addi-
tional pay. The Rabbi and Rebbitzin were assumed to be a "package
deal." Thus each time they moved Lillian too "lost her job" and had
to recreate it in a new place.

A Clergyman's Family

We really are just travelers
Who come, but cannot stay,
We linger long or sometimes less,
Then strain to be on our way.

Our house is borrowed for a while,
We're guests: but we presume
To look upon it as our own
And beautify each room.

We're transients, our bags half-packed,
We wait with moody mien;
Sooner or later the order comes
And we must move again.

Like Israel's ancient wanderers,
We pass from stand to stand;
Shall we someday put down our roots,
A home—our promised land?

Farewell to Sarnia
(Ontario, Oct 7, 1983)

We're on our way, so long, goodbye,
"We're here to stay" was just a lie
We told ourselves, and maybe you
Thought we'd stay forever too.

But we'll be gone before next Fall,
You'll miss us scarcely, if at all.
For in your inmost inner selves
You felt this energy won't last
If you're infused with zeal enough,
You'll rally round and strengthen ranks,
Forget the ones who let you down,
Regain your ground and carry on.

Eli on left; Lillian on the right with
Judy, Shu, David, and Rachelle.

101

Once Again

Once again our life stands still,
The pendulum hangs halting, limp,
It doesn't swing to left or right,
It sways in place ominously.

What's tomorrow? Here's today,
Blank as grey and cloudless sky,
Black as where horizon marks
The line of drab and flaky earth.

Spirits rise! Inspire and lead
Away from deep despair
Strike with vigor, bold and strong
Capture visions, eyes ahead.

Eli, Shu, and Lilllian on the movve from
Edmonton to St. Paul, 1960

Transients

Transients still as we have been
Since we met long ago
Just staying long enough to know
That we should move again.
Seeking always ideal grounds
To stake, perhaps to stay,
But though we've traveled South and North
East and now we're West,
Our eyes again are outward bound
Seeking where is best
To lead our straggling feet
And wishing but to leave.

To strike some solid roots
Before we go as everyman
The way of mortal flesh.
To make a greater imprint
Than we have heretofore,
To leave behind a golden link
Shiny, strong and firm,
A lasting gift, a loving ring
To help us feel secure
In knowing that the print we've made,
Won't quickly disappear.

We're Always in Between

We're always in-between
No stable home to call our own.
No roots struck deep
No planted trees to see mature.
No anchor firm
Just waved and tossed
From stem to stern.

No strong commitment anywhere
For fear we'd soon be thrust elsewhere
Just in-between the last and next
The present never sure, secure,
The past receding
Filmed in shadow
The future never fully grasped.

With van on hand
And books all packed
We're ready soon
To hit the track
A moving street
That points away
From where we've had
A short brief stay.

"Move on," an inner
Voice repeats.
Move on, move on
To other feats.
To other people,
Others' lives,
To touch the
Outward edge of joy
But not to taste it
Whole, full-blown,
Be quietly aligned with it.

A Clergyman's Destiny

We strike roots to be transplanted,
Blossoms sprout, we cut them short,
Stop your growth,
We're leaving soon,
To find another destination
To replant and start anew.

Now again we must start packing,
Once again it's time to leave,
So long, dear friends, good-bye,
Farewell.
We've stamped our mark upon your threshold,
Now we must go elsewhere.

So we pause at many stations
Barely resting body and soul,
Footsteps towards unknown horizons.
Pointed to uncharged goals.

I've lived so long with settling and moving
I'm always prepared to leave
In the back of me a metronome glides
It swings but is ready to halt
At the ring of a bell
The jar of a car

The muffled knock on the door
"Get thee out of this land —
Move yourself from this place.
We're sated with what you have done.
Your service is no longer
Needed by us.
On your way, then,
Leave and be gone."

After Arriving in Corpus Christie
(1983)

We've wandered again;
We're back to square one
With children to teach
And women to lead.

No anchor of place
No firmness of goal
Just plodding and slushing
And shuffling along.

Again I feel like a transient –
Here a week, a month, a year.
No home on this earth
That's our very own.
We'll wait for our share in heaven.

Why?

Why do I always want to go
To the places I've never been?
And why do I always want to see
The scenes that I haven't seen?

Why do I always crave to be
What I haven't been?
And why do I often tend to express
Thoughts that I really don't mean?

Why can't I simply be satisfied
To be in the place I'm in,
To limit my goal
For the sake of my soul,
Accepting of destiny's whim?

Lillian Levin Kahn, early 1960s

Shifting Sands

To journey far and then return
To sights that beckon twice
Is comforting till dawn appears
And then you realize
That home appears on shifting sands
Tomorrow it will slide
To other scenes and other views
No anchor there to point the way
You clutch at heaven's gems and stars,
They vanish with the dawn,
Your shadow and your echo hide
The ache that transience holds.

Nowhere

(New Castle, Pennsylvania, c. 1985)

I feel like a stranger wherever I've been,
The walls that surround me, the pictures, the art
Seem ready to fold and to fall far apart
Revealing stark space without sign-posts or
    marks,
Directionless, pointless
Which way to turn?
Forward or sideward,
Or straight up and out,
Away towards oblivion
Or reaching for stars.

Corpus Christi
(c. 1984)

Corpus Christi didn't excite me
Nor is leaving uninviting
But the manner of going
The anguish involved
The heartache and tension
And trauma
Lodge on the spirit
Like a layer of heat
Oppressive......

From the Frigid North

From the frigid North
To the sweltering South
And stations along the way,
We froze and we broiled
We shivered and sweated,
We longed for a singular day
When wherever we landed
Was perfect for resting,
For thinking and living and play.

Ode to a Small Town
(untyped)

Not like the odd, unfriendly pavements
    of the city.
Are your streets and roads
And paths that lead to home.

Not like the isolated one
Among the many
Is the feeling towards your neighbors.

Encounter

(c. 1958)

1.

Have you ever felt the magic lure
Of distant places, unknown climes
Intrigued, enticed by traveler's brush
Painting scenes both known and strange?
Enticed to cold and frosty North
Gateway to the great beyond
Boomtown of the shale and oil
Came the Jewish clergyman.

2

Jews lived there who struck their roots
In barren land, in virgin soil
And founded Synagogue and Schools
Remote from Jewish Center's pulse!

3.

By unseen bonds as strong as faith
By bridges spanning time and space
As durable as G-d's own love
Enduring as the Torah's laws
They cling unto the ancient truths
And build their Yavneh*[1] in the wastes.

---

1   Fortress of ancient learning established after Jerusalem was
destroyed

4.

Once more for skeptics' withering scorn
Toynbee's fossil rises, stirs
Ezekiel's dry bones line anew
And plant once more in foreign soil.
Their rigorous, vital heritage
Again the seed of Abraham
Draws sustenance from mystic springs
And is refreshed for future tasks.

5.

Keep faith, O nation, great though few
You G-d-intoxicated sons
Remember that your matchless past
Gives credence to your Father's love,
Keep faith in every land and clime
From frozen North to sultry South
Create new bonds of brotherhood
And links of gold to forge the chain
That stretches to eternity.

Dear Diary

(Before moving to Sarnia, Canada, Lillian stayed with her niece Rochelle Sobel and family in Potomac, Maryland, to continue in her job another eighteen months to qualify for a government pension.)

Sept 27, 1981

It's strange and unreal to be sitting here, Erev Rosh Hashanah[1] with no preparations to complete, no honey-cake to bake and no guests to anticipate—alone, without family—husband, children, or grandchildren for a yom-tov.[2]

A kind of numbness, overwhelms. Please G-d it shouldn't be like this again—so quiet—no anticipation, no excitement, no rushing to help you dear— didn't think we'd be a second Rosh Hashanah in limbo, but here we are—you, dear, are in Chicago—I'm happy though. Your being there gives Judy a place to be for yom-tov. ...

Oct 2, 1981

Rosh Hashanah has come and gone, a very strange and unreal holiday celebration for me, but I wasn't unhappy, I knew the future was ahead and it finally held a specific position, a real place—looking forward to abandon the limbo circumstances, no longer blowing in the wind.

But, as the Yiddish expression goes, every change comes with its difficulties and problems and for the moment this is arranging the moving

---

1   On the day before the beginning of the Jewish New Year.
2   Holy day

and facilitating its removal from local storage to a van headed for the Canadian destination. This phase is still in flux and hasn't been completed. So I sit and wait for the postman with the banker's check, for the call from Smith's Mr. Beam and for the next few days till I leave for Canada.

The Glass Half Empty

I Speak for Mediocre Man
(c. 1961)

I speak for mediocre man,
For him who seeks
To scale the heights,
Through word or song,
Or thought or deed.
But falters on the lower rungs.

I speak for mediocre man,
Who yearns to reach
The hidden spheres,
Leap far beyond the atmosphere,
Draw near to G-d's celestial throne,
Be tapped by immortality,
But stumbles in his fruitless search.

I speak for mediocre man,
His visions pierce through outer space
But he is shackled to the earth
A genius only in his dreams.

Unto Eternity
(untyped)

Each one lives a life of his own.
He alone and only he
Stands at his own particular
Point in the universe.
In a family, close-knit
Lives converge more often
Intimate, repeated, loving exchanges.
But each one lives a life of his own.
No two are ever the same.

Lillian, early 1960's.

Depression
(Untyped—old)

When youth and dreams make lithe your every
    limb
And boundless inspiration beckons far,
Then greatness lies just past the rising sun,
And creativity is yours to spare.

But quickly daily tasks absorb your years
And youth is spent while goals recede from sight.
Then fiercely leers the grim and awful truth
That greater ones have claimed the vision bright.

Suddenly the scene grows sharp and clear:
You share a mediocre way of life
With scores of people like unto yourself
Whose strivings hopelessly outstrip their lives
Who never reach the goals for which they strive.

Channels of my Mind
(untyped, after 1970)

The channels of my mind are closed.
Memory flees, elusive, blurred
Recedes before my shaky grasp
Mind is taut, the thought beyond
The view of understanding lies
Eyes gaze at an opaque veil
Behind which shadowy forms appear
With outlines that fade and disappear
Beyond the film of consciousness
Are pressing thoughts that beg expression
Pound the temples, cloud the eyes
Is that why I seek the sleep
Unto oblivion?

I stretch my hand to grasp, to reach
The depths of what I have forgotten
To plumb the deep unconscious of my mind
And drag forth memory
To return the past to me
So that I can peek ahead
And find a viable future.
If not I drown.

Sustain me, I faint.
Help me so that will may become deed
And in helping myself, I can give more
Than vocal response to others.

Channels of my Mind, in Lillian's handwriting

My Dream

I chanced to meet a fellow soul
In a strange, unlikely place,
Shafts of light were darting through
The slats that framed his face,

Spots of color—orange, pink,
And blue and purple too,
Shot up the wall behind his head,
His hair a motley hue.

"I come from distant points in space,
Beyond horizon's rim,
Come, explore the scene with me".
Should I have followed him?

Lillian before her marriage,
about 1940.

128

Sounds

Listen and hear
The sounds of a house,
Rustling, swishing, bang;
Creeping footsteps,
Muffled thuds,
Pierced by an unearthly screech;
Soft scraping fingers
Scratch like a cat
Prowling through whistling grass
Swoosh, do you hear?
The dark has a voice
That bounds from the bowels of Hell—
It frightens and weakens
Your heart and your knees,
You crouch and you shudder
You yell.
But none else has heard
The sounds that emerge
From the walls encircling your house,
The sounds that clutch
At your heart and your head
Shall I abandon my nerve-shattering house?

Contrast

He said:
"There must be some fun and some laughter,
Some levity and some guffaws."

She said:
"Laughter and fun are cruel and obscene,
In a universe peopled with flaws."

Said he:
"There must be some light-hearted banter
And frolic to soften the blows."

Said she:
"Frolic and banter are vicious and mean,
In a world writhing with woes."

On Aging

Lillian about 1941

Slipping

The years are slipping carelessly.
As they are wont to do.
We stand idly as they flee
Not knowing how they flew.

Then behold we reach a day
And stop quite frantically,
We try to halt onrushing time,
Unequivocally.

"What have we done to date," we cry,
"To warrant G-d's good grace?"
We set high goals we have not reached
To justify our fate.

Oh, rescue now my coming years
From bleak oblivion,
Unhand me from banality
My deeds with meaning crown.

Lillian with her husband Eli

135

Lament for Lost Youth

(untyped)

So engrossed with daily tasks
So wrapped up in our pointless lives
Are we, that seldom is there time
To gain perspective, grow, mature.

To us we seem to be as young
As spry as when we crossed our teens,
Until a jolt unlocks our soul
And contrasts us with youth today.

A pensive mood our mirror shows,
A sadness born of knowledge gained,
The light of truth reveals the lines,
Of age, of promise unfulfilled.

Where's the youth that spoke so grand
Of future effort, progress, growth?
'Tis late for us to change the years
So in our sons we seek the goals.

Welcome Death
(1960s)

If I were at the brink of death,

With only doctors to sustain me,
I'd want to die.

If I were hovering fitfully
From day to night, from life to death,
I'd want to die.

If I were knocking at death's door
I'd want no one with drug or balm
To make me live.

If wracked with pain
My body worn from illness and the prick of
    drugs,
If I were freely asked to choose
I'd want to die.

If death were standing at my side
And help was poised behind my bed,
I'd banish hope and voice my plea
"Oh, let me die!"

Wondering

What is the state in our existence,
When youth is gone and age is nigh.
We question, flounder, are unsure
Of everything we do or try.

The cockiness of youth has vanished
Age's calm is far away,
No longer are we sure and certain
Of anything we do or say.

We hover on the edge of bleakness,
We can't affirm, nor yet deny,
Our thoughts confused and very jumbled,
The road is dim, where do we fly?

Pansies
(May 1985)

There are pansies in the garden
And roses on the vines,
There is blooming oleander
And the greenness of the pines.
But the heart's no longer spring-like,
And the soul is not so bright,
The step is not so jaunty
And the spirit not so light.

Lillian's family about 1998. Left to right: Shulamit, Rachelle, Judy. Front: Rabbi Eli Kahn, Rabbi David Kahn.

Contrasts

I dreamed of robins gaily chirping,
Of pansies sweet and praying mantis,
But woke to see the falling snow
And winter on the branches.

I sensed my spirit fresh and gay
Free from pain and loss,
But the mirror showed a face
Wrinkled, lined with frost.

Memories

Memories recede,
Wane and fade,
Only impressions
Vaguely remain,
Like dents in a car,
Dissolving with time.

Shu, David, Rachelle and Judy on the steps of the
Indiana Harbor synagogue, 1958.

141

The Spring is Past

The years roll on,
The spring is past,
Autumn slowly creeps in view,
The air is chill
And laced with frost,
Sad, somber winter soon is due.

Hold back the days
As Joshua did,
Let the warmth pervade the air,
Stand still, my youth,
'Til worthy deeds
Create a cloak for cold's despair.

Memory

Your records say you're three score ten,
I see you through the veil of youth;
In vigor and in suppleness,
With handsome face and rapid gait,
With agile mind and spacious thoughts;
Memories cloud reality.

Rabbi Eli Kahn, age 80

On the Death of a Friend
(early 1970s)

Do not weep for me, my friends and dear ones,
Far greater men than I have crossed this bridge
And caused a void most difficult to fill
Yet, though their loss is vast beyond all thinking
Others stepped into their moral shoes
And carried on the chair of their traditions.

Do not weep for me, friends
My efforts circling all that I could give
Were scant and small
It makes no difference if I die or live.

Too Long

Too long we've lingered in this place
And seen its contours dim,
Too long shooed death from our embrace
And veiled our eyes from him.

Too long have we seen visions fade
And aspirations die,
Too long amid sorrow and the grave
Did goals and ventures fly.

Too long has winter chilled our hearts
With gloomy thoughts and schemes,
Too long has panic vised our soul
And frozen all our dreams.

Deliver us from hovering
Upon oblivion's brink,
Lift us up from dark despair,
O G-d, don't let us sink!

Unwanted

It's sad to contemplate the end
Of saint or sinner, foe or friend,
To know that as the shadows fall,
For hint there'll be no morn at all.

But worse by far than such a fate,
For anyone to contemplate
Is seeing death come riding high
And mortal flesh plead not to die.

To watch the struggle day by day
To know which one must needs give way
And yet defy the laws of death
When gone is all but faltering breath.

It's surely sad for anyone
To see bold death come strutting down
To stand aghast, but helpless, near,
Bereft of hope, devoured by fear.

Stations of the Past

The stations of the past are clouded over,
What's first, what's last I scarcely can perceive.
To some I said "Farewell," relieved with gladness,
For others deep ingrained I sadly grieve.
The stations of the past did vary greatly,
In goals and patterns, people, climate, size,
But always there were some to whom we
    mattered,
Who cherished us as sensitive and wise.

The stations of the past are clouded over,
Receding into memory's hazy zone,
Remote the scenes and friends we fondly
    gathered,
The present finds me visioning alone.

How Do I See You

He who sat with thoughtful men
And pondered metaphysics,
Now meets with little children
To teach the alphabet.

Yet the eager faces
Sit in adoration,
Sip the ancient culture
That sparkles from his lips.
That offer him fulfillment,
That affords him joy.

In them he sees the future,
His efforts of the moment
Will thus extend in time,
Reward him with contentment
Beyond this hour's grace.

Alzheimers

He once was full of wit and smiles and laughter,
His humor without guile charmed everyone,
Today his features frown with vacuous stares.

Yesterday he joked with friendly banter,
For vanity he turned his greying hair jet-black,
His form was tall, if not athletic.

Today his hair is white as shepherd's wool,
His mind is blank, his eyes weave back and forth
Like fleeing deer who know not where to go.

Once humor crinkled up his sapient eyes,
And lit his face with kindness and with joy,
Today his visage frames a ghostly pallor.

Is this the end of culture and of learning,
As this man sinks into dredging shoals of life
And wastes away propped up by false
    compassion?

If so, may death come gently to his weary soul,
Release his body from the hellish torment
Which stretches, stretches to oblivion.

The Hospital

This is a place of healing, you say,
Then why the drawn and sallow faces?
Why the fears that score the brow?
Why the hushed and saddened voices?
Why the harsh, oppressive pall
In this place that's made for healing?

Is this the place devoted to healing?
Then why does gloom pervade the air?
Why the cloud of suffering silence
The hint of doom, the bell that tolls.
Are illness and dying constant partners,
Here in this place of rest and repose?

Israel

The Wall

There it stands, a thing apart,
A viable structure, breathing clay,
Bigger than life,
Larger than imagination,
Its niches crammed with prayers and notes,
Its fissures filled with messages.

What caused hardened generals
To bow in deep humility,
And moved the impious soldier
To brush tears from his eyes?

This wall of layered bricks and stones
Holds secrets from long ages past,
Its mortar vibrant still today
Hides a prayer-shawl of sighs,
Petitions from devoted pilgrims
Who poured forth anguish, loss and pain
Stirred by strange and cryptic sounds
That echo from this mystic wall.

Israel

(For Independence Day)

A people and its land,
A nation and its soil
A State and its inheritance.

Not earth, nor trees and stones are these,
But history on every mound,
Memories in every rock,
Ancestors in every tomb,
Their deeds recounted year by year,
Their words enshrined in Holy Books;
Rock and hilt and soil alive,
Whispering secrets from the past.

Israeli Flag

Israel: Tribute to Ben Gurion

(Previously "Song of Hope", Published in the St Paul Jewish News 25 October 1963)

Israel stands alone today,
Perched on the brink of eternity,
Disaster pulses from the South,
Enemies poised to East and North,
Ready to sweep her into the sea.

Lesser ones have faltered,
Weaker states succumbed to dark despair,
Israel, though, stands firm and bold
Fortified by fearless courage,
Buoyed by boundless bravery.

Braced, sustained by countless martyrs,
By lofty goals to be achieved,
By four thousand years of history,
Four thousand years of a people's faith,
Myriad tears in a nation's past.

The road still rough and thorny,
The guideposts askew,
But the watchword
Forever and always
Spells "Hope[1]"

---

1   Israel's national anthem is "Hatikvah" which means "Hope".

David Ben Gurion, the primary founder and first Prime
Minister of Israel. (Photo: Haaretz)

Heavy Heart's Encased
(untyped, 1971)

My heavy heart's encased
As in a prison cell
And I myself am nailed
To iron prison bars.
But you, my blooming tree of life
Bend your twig towards me
Bursting with the ripened fruit
Of your hatred.
The dust transforms itself
On Sinai
And bones are clothed
With blood and flesh
On Sinai's heights
They stand silent in amazement
As a stone speaks to them
A speechless stone
On behalf of all the six million.
Lift up the rock
There's not a better weapon
O Sabra youth,
My longing and my hope
O Sabra youth
Encircled by fiendish fire
Where Jerusalem is severed

From the growth in the desert
Of the seared Negev
Life up the rock
From on the winding path
It is my heart
Wrenched from its sealed cage
It is the stone
Of David's victory.

Tenth Anniversary of Israel

(1958, Edmonton. Introduction to a much longer choral reading)

We rise to bless and celebrate today,
A nation's birth—a decade of development,
And thank Almighty G-d that we have
    lived to see
The flowering of a people's will
To freedom and to sovereignty.

On Poetry

Creations

I treat my poems
Like my children,
Neither cherishing
Nor coddling them.
I don't hover over
Or fondle them.
Mostly I ignore
Or even hide them,
But all the while
Fervently,
I beg of them to sally forth,
Sprout and blossom,
Grow and define themselves
To make me proud
And honored that they are mine,
Grateful that they exist
As loving, breathing, vibrant.
Vivid parts of me.

Elusive

What do you do when your mind goes blank
And your thoughts have taken wing?
When you labor for hours on simple sounds
That fade so you cannot sing.

What do you do when you stretch your mind
To grasp an elusive phrase?
When you seek an expression that's apt and right
Which hides beyond your gaze?

Go steal away,
Beyond the realm
Of conscience, and of men. Seek inspiration,
Ecstasy,
In fathoms deep within.

Reverie

Thoughts crowd in,
Not one is clear,
Jumbled,
Veiled,
Elusive,
Queer.

Then mind untangles,
Thoughts take form,
Lucid,
Sharp,
A poem
Is born.

Prayer

Dear Father, G-d, to Thee I pray
Not for peace of mind today,
Nor for wealth or length of days,
Not for power, nor for praise.

Only let me, G-d, create
A line, a thought, a song, a phrase,
That sparkles with Thy seal divine.
Then let me die.

Haiku's

The blue-black hair lay
Limp against the ashen face,
And then she sighed.

***

Boxes piled high one on one,
Winter came and summer's gone,
We're still here.

***

Blue-black hair and sad brown eyes,
Looking past the darkened night,
There she stands.

***

Hummingbirds with whirring wings,
Beat the air with cadence soft,
Then vanish.

***

The wind in the trees cries and moans;
Souls that mourn like the wind
Make me weep.

Heroic Couplets

Our sun that seers the grass and paints the face
Brings joy and harvest to another place.

***

While standing in that stark, ungodly light,
The vision of a spaceship came in sight.

***

It seemed as though the stifling midnight air
Weighed heavily on his soul and laid it bare.

Poems for Special Events

To My Daughter
(1990 after having forgotten Shu's special 40th birthday)

To make up for forgetfulness
Which strikes with passing years,
I send this loving tribute
To one we hold so dear.

This special birthday which we missed,
Passed up, forgot, ignored,
Does it reflect our latent wish
That birthdays be no more?

Perhaps we hope to hold the line,
Make fleeting time stand still,
And keep the years from pushing on
Too fast, against our will.

So with this poem and heart contrite,
With feelings deep, sincere,
We send our boundless love to you,
Throw kisses from afar.

May this year bring you happiness,
As well as years to come,
May pleasure, health, fulfillment, joy
Embrace your loving ones.

To My Granddaughter
(1992)

Ariella, you are six today,
The wonderment of school before you,
Glory in the new-found joy,
I'm sure your teachers will adore you!

Ariella Kahn-Lang at age six.

Tenure At Last

On the event of Shu receiving tenure in 1993

The news you told
Inspired me
(Although my form is slipping).
To pen this poem
Of Accolades
Deserved and highly fitting.
Intelligence and knowledge, too
And qualities of worth.
Indeed it is surprising then
Such honor was deferred.
All hail then to Tenure,
A prized and welcome goal.
We join with you to celebrate
This boon that feeds the soul.

To Devra Alexsandra, our First Bat-Mitzvah
(1987)

At twelve a Jewish girl, you know,
Approaches the threshold of maturity
Whose peak is only manifest
At forty
When our Sages say,
Understanding comes our way.
So Devra Alexsandra,
Beloved celebrant,
May you trod the path
Of devotion to G-d
And of learning and wisdom
Which Torah can bring,
Make the past vibrant,
The present assured,
The future a challenge
That strengthens your faith
And gives you the courage
To face all life's tasks,
Emerging triumphant
From trials and from pain,
Radiant and strong,
A leader among men,
As Devorah Haneveeyah,[1]
Whose namesake you are

---

1   The prophetess from the Book of *Judges* (chapters 4-5)

And gentle and modest
As loving and kind
As your grandmother, Devora,
After whom you are named.
May G-d keep you and guard you,
And bless you always,
Dear granddaughter Devra
Who brightens our days.

Devra Rosenfeld

To Devra

On the threshold of maturity
You proudly stand
With forward look
And steady eye.
The future spreads its colored strands
Which overlay the veiled events
That will emerge to crowd your life
And seek your choices, good or bad.

One last brief look
At childhood's ways,
One shouldered glance
At passing days,
Then turn your gaze
Ahead and high
And pray to be
Inspired and roused
By Jewish women, then and now
Whose love and zeal
For heritage
Enriched their days
And blessed their lives.

Look up and ahead!
Look up and ahead!
Devra Alexsandra, beloved b'chorah,[1]

---

1   Eldest female.

May G-d bless you and keep you
Today and always.
May you bring honor and joy
To those whom you love.

To Our Children
July 1, 1979

All the love we bear you, children
Often unexpressed and mute.
See it now to overflowing
In your warmly shared tribute.
Compassionate Judy,
Unpredictable Rocky
Witty Shu
And unworldly David,
Each one good and kind and fair,
G-d has showered blessings on us,
Children, such as you, are rare.

Each of you, unique and special,
Different from the other three,
How I love you each, my children,
As a group, and separately.

Then a new dimension followed,
Welcome sounds to charm our ears.
Dainty Devra,
Smiling Elana's "Saba, Sabta"
Brought happy tears.

Now this double "chai" you tender
With your love and your respect,
Bids us pause to thank our Father
Upon our blessings to reflect.

O our children, may He bless you
Guard you all in future ways,
And together may we savor
Smachot[1], joy in coming days.

Lillian with her children and grandchildren, 1988. Standing: David Kahn with daughter Fayga Malkah, his wife Sara Menucha with daughter Chana Raizel, Lillian, Shu Kahn and her husband Kevin Lang, Judy Kahn, Rachelle Kahn Rosenfeld, Eli Kahn; Seated: Yitzhak Kahn on Devra Rosenfeld's lap, Elana Rosenfeld, Ariella Kahn-Lang on Aliza Rosenfeld's lap, Chava Devorah Kahn.

---

1   Happy occasions

To Our Friend

Although our paths stretch far apart,
Lessie, you are in our heart,
And, though we can't in person join
In feting you with food and wine,
Our love, esteem and happiness
Is what we wish most to express.
May G-d watch over you and yours,
And bring you joy for many years.

Elfreda

There she stands so tall and slender,
Blue-black hair and sad brown eyes,
There she stands as I remember,
Statuesque, madonna-like.
Hair pulled back
Austere and taut,
Just a knot at nape of neck.
Regally she shifts her gaze
Toward the yellow irises,
Waving, swaying,
Standing tall,
They duplicate her
   charm and grace.

Lillian (left) with
Elfreda, 1956

Then she peers above, beyond,
Anguish fills her deep-set eyes,
In a fleeting, flashing glance,
She spies a tall and beckoning form,
Reaches towards him with her palm,
The vision fades, she drops her hand.

Winter Carnival

(early 1960s. Based on an item in the paper about 18 cases of frostbite from watching the St. Paul Winter Carnival parade.)

Sound the trumpet,
Pound the drum,
St. Paul's out
For winter fun.

King of Ice
And Queen of Snow
Make a cool,
Entrancing show.

Vulcan, Czar
of fiery might,
Prances skulking
Through the night.

Bu I, who rushed
To View this sight,
Now nurse a nasty,
Mean frostbite.

St, Paul Winter Carnival, St. Paul Minnesota

Reflections on Famous People and Events

A Question
(late 1950s)

The trees are grand for summer's shade,
Their green is lush, but cools the sight,
The bushes, flowers of every hue
Offer beauty and delight.

Will atom-splitting golems[1] crush
These witnesses of G-d's creation,
Transform them stark before our eyes
To chains of chemical relations?

The mushroom cloud of an atom bomb rises among
abandoned ships in Bikini lagoon, Marshall Islands, in this
July 1, 1946 file photo. (AP Photo/Joint Task Force One, File)

---

1   golem: a man-made monster

Grandma Moses
(sent to a poetry contest)

At eighty years your dormant soul
Woke to inspiration's call;
Art empowered your twisted fingers,
Untapped their former gentle strength,
So with your brush in gnarled hands
And youthful spirit as your guide
You sketched the scenes of memory.

The hidden layers of your brain
Now welled-forth
Like pent-up dams;
Releasing headstrong waves of mind,
The canvas shone with colors sharp
And vivid as the setting sun.

The cheerful, pleasant, simple folk
Strolling on their way to church,
Children laughing, mischievous,
Teasing running dogs and cats,
Suspended by your artist's hand:
One brief moment set in time
Forever vibrant and alive.

The Eichmann Trial
(sent to a poetry contest 1992)

Before the Bar of Justice
Humanity stood trial,
Before the Court of Heaven
Justice donned her veil.
All of us must shudder now
And weep with those who lived
Through tortured depths of horror
The mind can scarce conceive.

Defendant Adolf Eichmann takes notes during his trial in
Jerusalem. The glass booth in which Eichmann sat was
erected to protect him from assassination. (May 29, 1961).
(Picture from the USHMM Photo Archives, courtesy of the
Israel Government Press Office)

To Einstein

*(on viewing the Einstein sculpture in front of the
National Academy of Science, Washington, D.C.,
30 March 1992)*

To walk familiar through the paths of heaven,
To number planets, count the myriad stars
And graze the secret of the infinite;
To probe the mysteries of all creation
And in this knowledge
Marvel at the grandeur,
To see in awesome worlds and the atom,
The Hand of one All-Powerful creator;

For this your mind was cast in Adam's pattern
And rarefied with prophet's gift of knowing.
To leap into this age as one so human
Yet far above our simple comprehension,
One with us in body and emotion,
But near the throne of Heaven in lofty spirit;
Thus truly in accord with Holy Scriptures,
"In G-d's own form, O man, wast thou created."

Set amidst elm and holly trees on the grounds of the National Academy of Sciences, a 12-foot sculpture celebrates the life and legacy of scientist Albert Einstein. Einstein's bronze likeness, weighing in at four tons, is seated casually on a granite bench. The figure holds a tablet that lays out three of his best-known contributions to science. The sculpture was unveiled in 1979 in honor of the 100th anniversary of Einstein's birth.

Humility

A greater man 'twere hard to find,
Then Einstein, Light of humankind,
And one more humble or more plain,
Is rare indeed on any plane.
Simple people, on the other hand
Are sometimes vain and grandiloquent.

But have you thought, for one so great,
The humble cloak, the careless gait—
Garbed in a genius' piercing light
Which humility could never hide.
While we who stand aside in awe,
Must hide our defects and our flaws,

Space

Space!
Beyond the tug of earth's magnetic circle,
Beyond the ken of man's imagination,
Beyond the wildest, weirdest, rashest dream,
Space—fathomless space.

Who was with you on that journey
Superhuman astronaut?
Only G-d in stark infinity
What new worlds had you sought?

Assassination

(or "Shock", published, on the death of John Kennedy, November 1963)

The world stood still!
Then heaved a long, deep sigh
Of sadness, that shattered the silence
For one brief moment.
Ponderous oppression encumbered the day,
Heavily weighing on every soul.

The world stood still!
Breathing was inaudible,
Only sorrow had a voice,
Somber, stifled,
Grave, subdued,
Submerged in universal woe.

Heads of state and government,
Leaders, rulers, justices,
Ministers of every faith,
All enwrapped in solemn mien,
Bent of head
And bowed of heart.

Sad the day
And dark the hour,
Mournful now and evermore.

Shortly after noon on November 22, 1963, President John
F. Kennedy was assassinated as he rode in a motorcade
through Dealey Plaza in downtown Dallas, Texas.

A Year Later (To Esther)

(A year after takeover by terorists of the B'nai B'rith building when Norman Frimer was taken hostage, 1978. Rabbi Frimer was National Director of the Hillel Foundation. He was also the husband of Rabbi Kahn's sister Esther, Lillian's sister-in-law.)

I agonized with you, my sister,
Saw night fall and dawn arise,
Minus sun and minus light.
Avoiding sleep
Lest grief intrude,
Grief which shakes the inner soul,
Shatters hearts and captures thoughts,
Unstifled by the many calls
From friends and loved ones,
Silently a fervent prayer
That He who can program redemption,
Would bring us comfort and salvation.
Echoed from across the country
And beyond the distant seas.

I agonized with you, my sister,
Hung on every ether beam,
Haunted by the TV pictures,
Blurred and teasing,
Hurled from space,
Pounded by the radio men,

Hounded by the radio talk,
Sensitivity muted, lacking
In the search for more sensation,
When the facts so overpowered
Truth sought no embellishment.

I agonized with you, my sister,
And G-d was good and life still sweet,
And sweeter yet because it passed.
Through fiery furnace, hellish flames
Anguish recessed in the psyche
Revealed alone in hours like these,
Salvation kindling memory.

Norman Frimer, Deana Groengus (Binstock), Sam Bellows,
Esther Frimer, and Nina Bellows. The Frimer family still
celebrates the day Norman was released.

Carlebach

Forsooth, he cuts a sorry figure,
An aging guru, gills yet green,
Speaking still the speech of children,
Alone by children understood.

His once proud frame is bowed and withered,
Sad, indeed, his lingering note
Still stretching forth to reach the children,
Only they assuage his hurt.

Rabbi Shlomo Carlebach (1925-1994) is considered by many to be the foremost Jewish religious songwriter of the 20th century. In a career that spanned 40 years, he composed thousands of melodies and recorded more than 25 albums that continue to have widespread popularity and appeal.

The Rhythm of Jewish Life

Hanukah Thoughts
(c. 1992)

Still the flick'ring festive candles,
Mark the miracle of old,
Still the story of the grandeur
Is related and retold.

I have seen the eyes of children,
Not in Europe's ghettoed ways,
But in streets of freedom's cities
Sparkle, as they candle-gaze.

I have watched their ardent faces
Thrill to Maccabean lore,
To the tale of martyred Hannah
And the seven sons she bore.

Never will my people's future
Disappear from History's view,
While the eyes and hearts of children,
Keep it ever bright and new!

Once

Once upon a time 'twas said,
That Jews need suffering to live.
We scoffed at such absurdities,
And praised the vital Jewish soul.
Today it's quite another thought
That shakes and shapes our destiny.
It seems that only enemies,
Hostility and hatred voiced,
Can close our ranks
To act as one.

High Holy Days

Old traditions, ancient lore,
So, what are we trembling for?
Law of Moses, long since dead.
Why the awe and why the dread?

Though we've wandered far astray,
Regret, repentance rule today,
Divine the pattern; what a loss!
Our souls are dulled by daily dross

Once or twice or thrice each year,
Our inner Jewish souls appear,
We shed the bonds of work and strife,
Breathe a whiff of eternal life.

Heshbon Hanefesh[1]

This is the season of sifting and weighing,
This is the term for the searching of souls,
This is the moment of Heshbon Hanefesh,
This is the time for setting of goals.

How do we weigh and how do we measure?
How must we search our innermost self?
How fix the compass in proper direction?
How cleanse the spirit, restore it to health?

The answer is given; bold, terse, distinct:
Repentance and prayer and true charity
Give man the choice to think and to act
In freedom, averting the evil decree.

---

1   Means "taking spiritual inventory"

Sambatyon
(unfinished)

What turned my thoughts
To Sambatyon[1],
That river of myth and lore,
Which rages and storms
And thunders and foams
So no one can rest on its shore?
Except on the Sabbath,
When lo and behold,
A miracle comes to pass.
This roaring river,
Relentless and wild,
Is calm as the new-mown grass.

---

1   From a 9th century fable by Eldad the Danite, an itinerant
story-teller. The Sambatyon was a mythical river that protected the
Jews in an ideal land. Everywhere fruit trees were in blossom, and
the air was filled with a sweet fragrance. On three sides, the land
was bordered by the sea, and on the fourth side flowed a wide river,
the Sambatyon, in the midst of which boulders rolled and crashed
with a ceaseless thunder. For six days of the week, the rocks in the
river's midst continued their tireless churning. But on the Sabbath
they rested, and the river was as still and smooth as glass. To keep out
enemies, a curtain of fire arose on the opposite bank and remained
there until the following sunset, when the rocks resumed their
weekday commotion.

What Would You Do For Love?
(untyped, not old)

A glass of wine
And sweetened sauce
The twisted bread
Of Sabbath's fare
All your taste's desires are there
I set them down
To join with you
As we together, heart and hand,
Give thanks for our shared repasts.

Illustration from *Beyond the Sambatyon: the Myth of the Ten Lost Tribes*, published by MAXIMA Multimedia

How to Choose a Recipe

(sent to the Cooperative Consumer*)*

In the spring and summer my fancy usually turns to the testing of new and different recipes. The tastes of husband and children have become jaded and appetites satiated with foods and recipes that have been standbys for the long and fierce Minnesota winters. It is then, when spring fever is at its height, that I seek to relieve the tension in a delightful and satisfying way be seeking out the recipes from the national contests and from new books that magically appear on the market at this time.

For other women, a new spring hat does the trick. As for myself, I must examine a hundred and more interesting or provocative recipes, buy new and unusual ingredients, and go on a recipe-testing binge.

Do I ever choose new recipes for my file, or do I find that the tried-and-true ones are still the best? Of course, I select new ones. I'm somewhat of an iconoclast, not in the field of faith, where I am a devout believer, but in such areas as recipe collecting and recipe testing. Here I may throw out old and used recipes, air out the file and insert some brand-new, fresh ideas for the hands and for the mind, as well as for the taste.

And how does one go about making this revolution in the recipe box? It is simple, indeed! Where home-baked pastries are concerned, my

Lillian at her Passover table.

family enjoys anything with chocolate or something especially dainty or different. Often, I've perused twelve and fifteen recipes from the national contests and only chosen one for experimentation. On the other hand, I've sometimes found a whole useful column in my favorite newspaper.

But above all, I've had great luck at teas for ladies, particularly in Western Canada, where we lived for several years. There, every recipe was a gem and I'm still testing some of the superb ones I picked up from these home-making minded women and from the tested recipe booklets printed by some church groups and women's organizations.

As for main dishes and desserts, the field is so wide and diversified that one doesn't know where to begin and what to eliminate. In this area, I run the gamut of experimentation from fixing meats with new herbs and piquant sauces to preparing airy and light summery desserts that intrigue the sight and tempt the palate.

There is, however, one hard and fast rule from which I never depart. We have a family of four children and, as the wife of a clergyman, I am involved in numerous activities that demand time and effort. Besides, we often have many guests or out-of-town company with whom I must maintain a culinary reputation. I, therefore, seek recipes with all of the above-mentioned qualities, but with one added virtue—simplicity. They must have directions easy to follow and must be simple to concoct. Surprisingly enough, some of the best recipes I have tried and used with repeated success are the ones that need little time and effort to prepare. They seemed intricate and difficult, but had a subtle simplicity that was only revealed when I received requests for the particularly appetizing dish or dessert.

I pass on these hints to busy homemakers like myself, who enjoy being creative in the kitchen, but who have limited time and limited patience with which to carry out their duties and desires.

Pirkei Avot
(Ethics of the Fathers)

(1972, for a script called "What is Judaism?")

Tradition

(Pirkei Avot 1:1)

Tradition teaches many things,
Of what is past and what's to be.
It serves as anchor to our lives,
Gives them meaning, quality.

Moses, Joshua, then the Elder,
Next the Prophets form the chain
All the Great Assembly follow,
Then scholar, teacher, saint.

Lillian the Rebbezin (on left), 1960

Three Crowns
(Pirkei Avot 4:17)

There are three crowns a man can wear,
Adornments brilliant to the view,
The Crowns of Torah, priest or king,
That gain applause and praise where due.

But one crown bright as dawn itself,
Always fresh as spring's first rain,
Cannot be sought from lineage
Or bought and kept by money's gain.

This – the crown of one's good name,
Lasting more than lifetime's span,
Outshining birth and wealth and fame,
Forever set in hearts of man.

If You Would be a Scholar
(Pirkei Avot 2:5)

If you would be a scholar
Or a learned Jew
Then daily when you plan your work
Make time for study too.

If Not for Myself

(Pirkei Avot 1:14—"If I am not for myself, who is for me? But if I am only for myself, what am I? And if not now, when?")

I must be firm,
I must be true
Unto myself.
If not I, who?

But if I think
Of self alone,
How sad indeed,
When all is done.

And if not now
To do what's right
To help a man
In sorry light.

And if not now
To soothe the ache
Of troubled souls,
Of hearts that break.
And if not now
To heal the scarred
The one whose life
By pain is marred,
Yes if not now,
Then when?

Keep Three Things in Mind
(Pirkei Avot 3:1)

If you desire to ward off sin
Just keep three things in mind:
A Universal Eye looks on,
A Listening Ear takes heed,
A Moving Finger silently
Records your every deed.

What is the Course?
(Pirkei Avot 2:1)

What is the course that one (you) should choose
In traveling on through time
To reach the straight and righteous way
That makes one's life sublime?

The path that offers self-respect
And brings us only praise
From others, is the one to take
And follow all our days.

Make a Fence About the Torah
  (Pirkei Avot 1:1)

"Make a fence about the Torah,"
Our ancient Sages taught,
To keep the Law intact
And guard it well, in thought and act,
Observe it as you ought.

You'll treasure each and every word
The Law is precious unto you.
This stamp of truth will be your plan,
This seal of G-d's belief in man,
The heritage of every Jew.

Do Not Say
(Pirkei Avot 2:5)

Do not say, when I have time
I'll study and I'll learn
The sacred works of Jewish lore
The books to which we turn
For inspiration and for goals,
Ideals toward which we yearn.

Perhaps you'll never have the time
In future as today,
So read and study now, dearest child,
Gain wisdom while you may.

Do Not Be Like Servants
(Pirkei Avot 1:3)

Do not be like servants
Who serve a master well
For wages or for prizes
Or for a place to dwell.

But rather be like children
Who look upon their G-d
As Father, from whom all they want's
A kind approving nod.

Lillian Kahn (on right) directing a play in her role as program director and Rebbezin.

Hillel

(Pirkei Avot 1: 12)

Of gentle scholars none so great,
And none so meek as Hillel,
Whose words of wisdom always teach,
Whose acts of kindness serve to preach,
Concern for every man.

Who is Lucky
(Pirkei Avot 4:1)

Who is lucky?
He who finds
The good in life
And peace of mind.

Who is wealthy?
One who knows
That wealth can come
And wealth can go.

Who is happy?
He who feels
G-d's goodness is
To him revealed.

Consider That
(Pirkei Avot 1: 6)

Consider that your fellow-man
Depends on you to understand
So judge him kindly, treat him well
And favor him on every hand.

Know Before Whom
(Pirkei Avot 3:1)

The wise man thinks of many things,
But three you all should know:
Reflect from where and whence you came,
Consider where you go.

Above all else, remember this
Account of deeds you owe
To Him, we call the Lord of all
Who leads this earthly show.

Study Torah
(Pirkei Avot 2:2)

Study Torah all your days,
But keep this thought in mind
To spread its teaching far and wide
Practiced by all humankind,
You must in all your daily tasks
Not leave its truths behind.

Torah studied every day
Becomes worthwhile and firm
If daily occupation tends
To strengthen what you learn!

Lillian Levin Kahn, 2013

www.ingramcontent.com/pod-product-compliance
Lightning Source LLC
Chambersburg PA
CBHW060046100426
42742CB00014B/2718